THE
SIX FIGURE
NETWORK MARKETER

Volume 1

CHRISTOPHER COLE

The Six Figure Network Marketer Blueprint
VOLUME 1

The Essential Guide That Can Take You From Zero To Six Figures in the Network Marketing Industry

Christopher Cole

Copyright © 2020 Christopher R Cole

All rights reserved.

ISBN: 978-0-578-73802-4

CONTENTS

Introduction - The 3 Biggest Issues People Have With Network Marketing   1

Chapter 1   The Pain of Running Out   10

Chapter 2   High Quality Prospects   15

Chapter 3   Creating Attraction   22

Chapter 4   Create Your Tribe   29

Chapter 5   Increase Those Volume Points   36

Chapter 6   Content That Matters   40

Chapter 7   Funnel Them In   50

Chapter 8   It's Going Down in The DM's   54

Chapter 9   Master Duplicator   64

Chapter 10   Become A Product of Your Product   68

Chapter 11   Autopilot   73

Chapter 12   You're Not Alone Anymore   77

BONUS Ultimate Hack Action Items   82

To All Network Marketers

PREFACE

I USED TO BE RIGHT WHERE YOU ARE AT THIS VERY MOMENT. I ALSO DECIDED THAT I WOULD MAKE A CHANGE. THIS IS YOUR CHANCE TO CHANGE YOUR LIFE FOREVER....

Read this before you begin the book!

The 3 biggest issues people have within network marketing are recruiting, sales, and duplication. I am going to share a simple solution to help with each of those pain points that most network marketers have to overcome. I am also going to invite you into my private Facebook group where you will have access to more detailed information on overcoming these roadblocks. They only take a small amount of time to add to what you are currently doing or are not doing. You'll see some incredible results fast. Within your first 30 days to be exact. But you have to put in the work and do them exactly as I share. So stick around. Read the book. I'm looking forward to educating you and sharing my secrets with you. I am here for you. That's why I'm doing this. I care about your success.

At this point, I am sure you are asking why now? Why am I writing this book? It is because things are changing. Everything is going more online. This could be a vital tool for the growth of your network marketing business. With this transition, you want to be able to run your business from home and automate it. You enrolled in a home-based business. That's why now. A lot of things and trends are going online and network marketing is going to be one of those opportunities. The industry is going to be bigger than it already is and I want you to take full advantage of that with these tools so you can inspire and change more lives, as well as your own. You have to be ready for the change that is coming and with these tricks and tools you can continue to grow faster than you ever have before. Being adaptable is one of the greatest skills you can have in this industry. If you do not have that skill then things are going to change without you growing. Be willing to change with the times and the technology that is being created right in front of us at this very moment. There are so many social media platforms and different ways we can communicate.

Let me ask you this. Why are you here? Why are you reading this? I know you are looking for clarity. You are looking for help. You are looking for someone to pull you up. I understand because I have been exactly where you are. Before, I had no direction. I was simply told to figure it out. I was told to follow these simple steps when starting out. But those steps don't work for everybody, especially if you are starting with a small network of friends. You can look up to me as your up-line leader. I will help give you the direction and clarity you need to have the success that you want. We will conquer this mountain together. My private Facebook group will also be open to you and will always be a place you can come for direction and clarity.

https://www.facebook.com/groups/The7figurenetworkmarkete

Introduction:
I have Felt Your Pain and Frustration

You picked up this book because you are looking for answers. You want to know the secret. You are ready for success. You want to pass your up-line. I get it! I was there. That six figure a year goal is calling your name. You ask yourself how could you ever get to six figures in the network marketing industry. I know that I wanted to reach that point because I wanted to go full-time in the industry. I wanted to gain the freedom that everybody says comes with network marketing. The time freedom. The wealth that you could create for you, your friends, and family. You want more time with your family. You want to go on vacation with your friends or family when you choose to. You want to reach $10,000 a month. This is all possible for you if you want it as bad as you tell yourself you do. I am going to call you out on that and say that you have to want it so badly that you cannot wait to wake up the next day to take massive action! That you have to be willing to give up certain things for a short amount of time to reach that goal. But what is more important to you? What are you going to decide?

You could have picked this book up because you're interested in the opportunity. You are seeing what may be possible for you. The top 1% of that network marketing company that you are in is where you want to be. You want to be the success story in your company.

You want to be on stage and inspire others to make the change needed to be a success in network marketing.

Or maybe you're someone who has already been in the industry for a while, but you're trying to figure out better ways to help your team grow. To help speed up growth through the compensation plan. I am telling you it is possible. Changes are happening right in front of you and you might not even realize it yet. Maybe you have. I know you have seen the ads on Facebook about recruiting online or getting more leads online the non-traditional way. The internet is here to stay, but are you?

Times are changing. But are you? Are you ready for the growth that is going to happen in the industry? With all that is going on, you have to be ready for the change that is going to happen. A lot of business will be moving completely to social media. I am going to help prepare you for that change. I am going to share simple steps you can take to increase engagement, sales, and duplication, and to grow your network marketing business on Facebook. All of the other platforms are great also but I truly believe Facebook is the best place to start. If you have a massive following already, GREAT. Let's start that Facebook group and maximize the following that you do have for your opportunity. No time to not have all areas covered.

It took me a while to have success, and that is one of the reasons I wrote this book. My goal for this book is to help speed up your success. I do not want it to take you a long time to reach your goals and get to the top 1% of your company. I do not want your growth in the business to be slow. I want you to impact more lives faster because that is why you got into the network marketing industry to begin with.

The impact can happen in your own life as well. You can go full-time and reach six figures within the network marketing industry. You can step away from whatever you might be currently doing to go full time within the industry. Even if you want to stay part-time, you can still reach six figures. It is possible. With a strong work ethic, dedication, and time, you can get there. I want you to get there.

You may be wondering who this guy is who is telling you what you deserve. My name is Christopher Cole. I am 34 years old and I am from a small Midwest town in Ohio. I grew up in a typical middle-class family, and we had everything. My father had a bunch of businesses and my mom was a stay at home mom. Up until the age of 18, I had a pretty good, normal life. Then we had a major event that changed our family forever. My father got charged with embezzlement. We lost everything. I remember coming home on my last day of high school and turning over the keys to the car that I had. We had to pack up everything we owned and move out. We had no idea what we were going to do next. I was so scared at this point. I was broken also. I did have some great friends that helped me through this tough time. So did my amazing grandparents in Pennsylvania. I also want to point out that my amazing mother helped us all make it through this tough time. I would not be writing this book either if it was not for her constant belief in me and what I decide to do. I love you Mom.

I wanted to go where I knew opportunity was, and the closest major city to me was Columbus, OH. It is a college town and the opportunities were endless.

My brother was in college at Ohio State University, so I decided to move up to the city of Columbus with him. I did not know what was next for me. I had no idea what I wanted to do. I planned to take the traditional route and go to college, get a degree, get a good job, and start a career. But I quickly realized that was not the path for me. I dropped out after my first semester of college. I realized that I wanted to start a business of my own, be my own boss, and earn what I was worth. That's when one of my best friends introduced me to the industry of network marketing. The best opportunity for me that did not need a lot of money to start was a network marketing business. That is how my journey in the industry started.

As I dived into network marketing, I lucked out. My best friend Ryan and his dad Bill were already a part of a successful network marketing company. His dad started earning six figures in that company back in the '90s. I moved again back to Zanesville, OH where they were living at the time. Ryan and I would do weight loss challenges out of his dad's gym that he owned and the business was growing, but I got discouraged because I felt like I was a burden on them since I was not having massive success with it from the start. If that is you as well, I want you to know it's okay. That's why you are here reading this book. I was truly grateful for them and still are today.

But my luck did not last long. In the first three years, I had very little success. I felt like I could never reach that pivotal six figure income and go full-time with the industry. So, to be honest, I got burned-out and decided to step away from network marketing. This is something we are not going to let happen to you.

I went on a journey of self-discovery and tried a bunch of other things. I did a lot of sales jobs, went to college for a year, and did other random things, trying to figure out what to do with my life. I had no direction. I had no purpose. I was depressed. I went through a lot of ups and downs, desperate to figure out what I truly wanted out of life. Throughout this entire period, I kept following my friend and his dad. They were doing incredible things with the first opportunity I signed up for. So, I swallowed my pride after six long years and got welcomed back with open arms. Unfortunately Ryan's dad, Bill, passed away, but his legacy still lives on through Ryan, his family, his team, and the opportunity I am still a part of to this day. That's one of the most incredible things to me with this industry, that you can create a legacy and it can live on through you and your family. I dive into more of that in a later chapter.

NOW it gets interesting. I got tired of being down on myself. I got tired of wanting more without taking action to get to the palace I wanted to be. I knew that life is short and very precious. That you cannot get time back. That I had to make a decision to be ALL IN on my life because no one else would be.

I decided to get serious because it's a serious business. Within three years of being back, I was making six figures a year. It took a lot of dedication. A lot of time and growth. A lot of personal development. A lot of mental clarity. A lot of drive. A lot of education.
A lot of failures. I have all of this stuff that I've been able

to compact into 10 years of experience. It has not been an easy journey, but it has been worth it. The growth has been worth all the pain.

Chapter One

The Pain Of Running Out

Are you confused about how to recruit? Are you always frustrated because you are doing exactly what your up-line said to do with no results? Does everybody keep telling you it's a pyramid scheme? Do you lock up and get nervous when speaking to someone about your product or opportunity? I have experienced all of these when I first started in the network marketing industry. You no longer have to worry about that. With what I am going to teach you, you will be recruiting your ideal client and distributor in no time. Recruiting is an art and you must learn to master it if you want to have success in the industry. I know you can do it because I learned how to do it and I was awful when I started. I also used to beg people to join my opportunity, just like you may be doing. We are going to equip you with the tools that will not require you to do that.

Do you know who or how to figure out who your ideal client or distributor is? If not, that's okay. I am going to help you figure that all out step-by-step. In network marketing, you are able to choose who you want to connect with. It does not matter how far along you are at this point, you will likely have someone who you can connect with deeply. These are the people you would consider your best friends. People you know right away will be important in your life.

When I first started my network marketing business, I would recruit just about anyone. I did not believe that I could recruit the perfect customer or distributor for my business. I was wrong. These are the people that have already made up their minds to make a change. They are highly driven individuals. They are looking for everything that my opportunity offers, and they have the money to get started.

I proved to myself that I was wrong. As I started to speak directly to my ideal client, I noticed instant results. I started to have more growth, more engagement, and more sales. With doing this repeatedly, I was able to increase clarity and understanding. The first step of understanding how to get to six figures in network marketing is to understand who your ideal client is.

Recruiting is one of the major skills that you must learn to build a team of distributors. Without recruiting you have no business. I am sure the way you learned to recruit was to reach out to everybody you know right away. To have a home party. To set up three way calls. To go public on your Facebook page. To add random people on Facebook and message them right away when they accept your friend request. This is the old way of recruiting. You will never have to do these awkward ways of recruiting again. What if I told you that you never have to run out of people to talk to again? You would think I am crazy. But it's true.

HOW TO:
    1.) Practice.

    2.) Master the skill.

    3.) Figure out your recruiting style.

The Six Figure Network Marketer

> **YOU CAN BUILD THE LIFE YOU WANT**
>
> —CHRISTOPHER COLE—

Chapter Two

High Quality Prospects

One of the biggest issues you seem to hear people have with network marketing is running out of people to talk to. However, there are so many people on social media. You just have to know how to find them. In this chapter you are going to find out how it's possible for you to never run out of leads again. I will also teach you how to increase your engagement on Facebook by as much as 300% in 30 days. This whole book is going to be focused on the social media platform Facebook and how you can generate leads and increase engagement. You will be able to take this information and use it with your whole team. Facebook is a free platform, so why not take full advantage? I will explain to you the exact steps that you will need to take for you to see results. You must follow these steps exactly as described or you will not see results.

My mentor, Ryan Niddel, said you have to think of Facebook as an auditorium. You have 5,000 seats in the auditorium. 5,000 because that's the largest number of friends that you can have on Facebook at any given time. You don't want people on your Facebook page that are not your ideal client or customer. It's your business storefront. You don't want to have people who are not willing to buy from you taking up space. It's the same when it comes down to whatever network marketing company you are in. You don't want to have all your spots taken up by people who are already in the same company as you. Instead, have them follow you on a different platform like Instagram. Do the opposite of everyone else. Protect your store front of 5,000 people. Be the bouncer of your Facebook store front and only allow in people that want to buy from you and be your customers, or work with you. Those that have a credit card ready to buy from you to gain access. Be smart, be intentional, and set standards. This is one of the most important things you can do when it comes to getting to six figures in your network marketing business. I know you want to be nice, but when it comes to this, it's something you have to protect. It is a part of your business and that is your source of income and success.

HOW TO: Friendfilter.io.

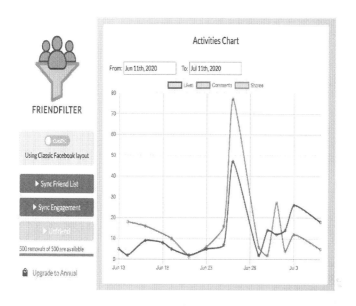

One of my favorite secret tools that I learned about from my mentor is called Friendfilter.io. This incredible tool will help you clear out all of the people that are not engaging with you on your Facebook page so you can focus on the friends that do. You want a platform that has a lot of engagement and this makes it super easy to create that space.

The first time you run this, you only want to remove 200 friends a week. No more than that because Facebook will lock up your account. You will want to repeat this every 30-60 days depending on how many of your ideal clients you are adding. This process is going to take some time, but it will put you in the position to make a lot of easy sales and increase the recruitment of your ideal client.

The goal is to get to 5,000 of your ideal clients or potential distributors. Even if you got to 1,000 of your ideal clients, this would do so many incredible things for your business. You would no longer have to beg people to buy your products or beg them to join your opportunity.

This will take some time to finish, but don't let that discourage you. Know the reason why you are doing it. It's going to make everything easier for you and for your team when you teach them this.

Action Items for High Quality Prospects:

1.) Visit https://friendfilter.io/

2.) Sync Friends List- This is free to do.

3.) Sync Engagement.

4.) Clear our 200 Friends max a day that are not engaged.

5.) DO NOT DELETE all in one day.

6.) Add your Ideal Clients Daily (20-40 New).

7.) Repeat steps until you get to 5,000 of your Ideal client.

You may need some help with this process. Inside of my private Facebook group, I have a video to help walk you through this process step-by-step.

https://www.facebook.com/groups/The7figurenetworkmarketer/

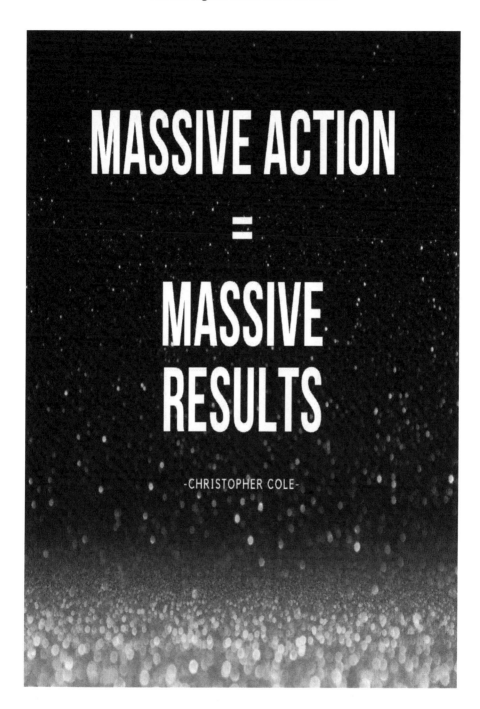

CHAPTER THREE

CREATING ATTRACTION

Create engagement with a conversation starting post. This post can be about anything that you choose, but it should be about something that starts conversation. You can't be attached to what people say because everybody has different views on things. It's more so about the engagement that you are getting on that post. You want to make sure you are responding to their comment with a question to keep the conversation going. Make sure to click the heart button. These two steps are so important.

HOW TO: The Noise Canceling Message.

What I mean by having a noise canceling message is that you want to have a message that stands out. A message that cuts through all the spam. It's going to set you apart from everybody else. My noise canceling message is, "I help motivated network marketers increase their profits by as much as 200% in as little as 30 days so they can move at their marketing plan faster and create higher quality leads." That's what I'm known for doing well and it's efficient. Now it's time to figure out your noise cancelling message. You have to zone in on that. What do you want others to know you for doing well? What message are you going to have that will help your noise canceling message stick out. No one is doing this right now and that gives you the advantage in your marketplace. Be different. Do what the others are not doing.

There are few ninja secrets that my mentor taught me that have helped my business explode, and I would like to share them with you. The first one is called priming the pump. Every morning for 15 minutes you want to interact with other people's content. Hit that love button and engage and converse with them. Be interested, be real, be genuine. Respond to their content with an honest question about it. The goal here is to help you build a relationship with them. This is one of the many reasons why people fail in network marketing. They always try to sell, sell, sell. So take a step back and start taking a genuine interest in the people you are friends with. It is the same as how I care about you.

Do this process consistently, every morning, for 30 days straight and you will be thrilled with your results. But remember, this only works if you follow the steps exactly. Build that client base. Build that potential distributor base. Increase engagement with other people and add value. When somebody does add you as a friend, PLEASE don't go into the inbox right away. Don't be like the 95% of network marketers that look desperate. You have all experienced that and it's the wrong way to do things. Go to their wall and engage with their posts. Let them know you care about what they are posting. Build a relationship. Building a relationship is the most important thing that you can do. Don't make the mistake of asking for the sale right away like a lot of network marketers do. No one wants to get sold. It's a turnoff and it's not the way to do it.

Action Items for Creating Attraction:

1.) Clean up your Facebook. Become attractive.

2.) Does your Facebook profile picture look professional?

3.) Would you buy a product from you?

4.) Take this time to change your profile pic. (If you have an iPhone I suggest getting a friend to take a nice photo of you in portrait mode).

5.) Take this time to change your cover photo also. (Quick tip: look at your profile on your mobile device. If you can clearly see both photos it's done).

6.) If you don't have any professional photos it's okay. They don't have to be perfect. Just better.

The Six Figure Network Marketer

> **THE DREAM LIFE YOU WANT IS WAITING ON YOU**
>
> —CHRISTOPHER COLE—

Chapter Four

Create Your Tribe

Facebook groups can take your ideal client from cold to warm. What that means is taking someone from not wanting to buy anything from you to wanting to buy something from you. Create a Private Facebook group that caters to your ideal client. Whether it be other network marketers that you're trying to help or if it's for your team. I would do both. Make it a private group. The secret is setting the standard for your group and the mission of that group. You want to add a welcome video and pin it to the top of your group page. In the welcome video, you want to set the standard for what to expect in that group right away and stick to those standards. Don't let other people try to cross recruit in your group. Always be in Facebook groups to help lift each other up. There is so much more I can teach on this but I'm only giving you the starting steps.

You should be posting in your group five times per day. You also want to go live in your group every day. You have to stay engaged with the group. Offer weekly meetings that you can answer any questions anyone may have. Be personable, share your personal story, and build closeness with the group.

HOW TO: Facebook Group Creation and Set-up.

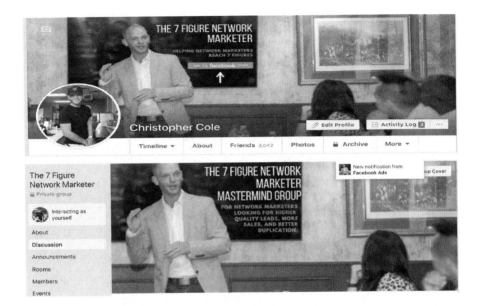

When setting up your private Facebook group, you want to make sure that it has the same feel as your personal page. I did not mention this earlier but I will now. You can visit my Facebook page and see how I have my profile picture and cover photo set up. You want it to look professional, and make sure that when you are on a mobile device you can read everything well. This is because most people are on their cell phones when looking at who you are and what you represent. You don't want to cause confusion with what it is that you do. This is so important because what I see a lot of network marketers do is not have a photo of themselves. People will automatically think you're a scam right away. That will not help your business grow at all.

Be the gatekeeper of your private Facebook group. You are allowed to add questions for people to answer when you are allowing access to your group. You don't have to allow every single person into your group. Know your ideal client and only be inviting them or allowing them into your group to become a part of your tribe. You will want to provide some value at all times in the group. As I mentioned previously, you will want to create a welcome video and pin it to the top. You can find more information on what this looks like in my personal private Facebook group.

Everyone wants to feel special in your group. Like I stated, Facebook allows you to ask three questions to anyone who asks for permission to join your group. These questions can create massive value in your future. The three questions I would have you post are as follows. These are questions my mentor constructed and they have proven to work time and time again.

1. Welcome to [group name]. We're excited to have you here! There is no shortage of [ideal clients] waiting to come into the group, so an incomplete request will be denied. Do you agree?

And then hit the option "required" next to it so people see it.

2. What is the largest pain point that exists inside of your [ideal client] world?
For example, my question is, "What's the biggest roadblock inside of your coaching business? Would you like help moving it out of the way?"

That is also required.

3. Where can I send (information and marketing)?

The third and final question is aimed at getting their email address. I say, "Would you like a personalized video introduction?"

Action Items for Creating Your Tribe:

    1.) Create a Private Group Page (Your Name).

    2.) Create a Welcome Video (Share your story).

    3.) Pin the video to the top.

    4.) ONLY invite people to the group that have responded to your product or opportunity Engagement post.

5.) Post five times a day in your group (Product info, Client testimony, Promotion, Live).

6.) You must go live in your group one time per day. Just share a day in the life of YOU.

Chapter Five

Increase Those Volume Points

I know what you're feeling and I have been there. Not being able to have enough sales and having a slow sales cycle. Having to beg people at the end of the month to buy something from you. Having to create a list of 100 people. It's not an attractive way to build a network marketing business. It's stressful and it's awkward. I am going to teach you a way that you never have to beg someone to make another sale again. A way that will have your ideal client asking you to buy your products. This was the greatest feeling when it started to happen for me. It was a very pivotal change for my business and my team's business. I was able to teach them exactly what I am going to show you. You can duplicate this and I suggest that you do, so you can create that story for the stage! Imagine the feeling you are going to have when this changes for you? Imagine what your volume is going to look like with this change.

You will be able to connect with your exact client. You will have people asking if they can buy from you. In this chapter, I will teach you what to do when you don't have enough sales or when you're not hitting your goals. In order to be successful, you must have some form of automation. A consistent cycle of posting about you using your products, results you have achieved from using your products, and your customers' results from using your products.

This is not what you should be posting every single day on your personal page. You will want to increase your engagement also for your products. What noise canceling message can you create to help sell more products? It's crazy to me because when you get into the industry your up-line has you do that 100 person list right away. However, your up-line didn't have success with it, and they want you to do it and see if you have success with it. It doesn't work, it's overwhelming, and it's outdated. I don't want that to be overwhelming for you. I want you to love this industry and enjoy being in it, so a stress free sales cycle is what I am going to help you do. It will take 30-60 days to start seeing results, but it's also highly duplicable.

Actions Items for Increasing Those Volume Points:

1.) Personal Page - Share your personal health testimony one day per week.

2.) Get a NEW result or be working on one.

3.) Be OPEN and share photos (I know it's uncomfortable).

4.) GO LIVE.

LEAVE THE PAST IN THE PAST AND FOCUS ON THE FUTURE

—CHRISTOPHER COLE—

Chapter Six

Content That Matters

You have to create a content calendar, and in my private Facebook group, The 7 Figure Network Marketer, you will have access to one. You have to set yourself up for success. Once you have it mastered, then you will be able to hire a virtual assistant that can help run all of this for you. We will save that secret for another book. Or, join our incredible supportive community on my Facebook page where you will have access to many great resources and will have the opportunity to schedule a one-on-one call with me to brainstorm.

First, lead with the products. Not the opportunity.

What I mean by lead with the product is don't lead with the opportunity. This is where the current industry has it all wrong. You first must get a result from your product. If you don't have a result from the product you represent, then you have no story to sell. You want to package a story that you can share with others. This is so important, especially if you're new to the industry. If you've been in the industry for a long time, you need to get a new result. Take the time to create your story. Document it every step of the way. You have to get out of your comfort zone when it comes to this. All the amazing things that can happen for you are on the outside of that zone you are so comfortable and stuck in. WHO CARES what others think. This is your life, your journey, and your business success story! Facts tell, stories sell.

HOW TO: Create Content Calendar

Now, keep in mind, this doesn't cost you any money, but it will cost you some time. The investment is certainly worthwhile, as just this strategy alone has helped myself and many of my clients hit $10,000 per month inside of our network marketing business online. We are going to start with something that I refer to as a content calendar. How much easier would it be if you knew every day exactly what to post, how to post it, and why you are posting it? This was extremely overwhelming for me. I never knew what to post and exactly when to post it. We forget just how easy it can be to make an impact in the marketplace, and that's what the content calendar is all about. All this I am sharing about the content calendar was shared with me by my mentor.

MONDAY MONDAY

So we're going to start on Monday, and Monday is used for an engagement post. This engagement post should be typed, not a video or a picture. The engagement posts should fit in one of the nice colorful backgrounds on Facebook or on one page inside of Instagram. Typically, open-ended questions are the best. For instance, "Where would your favorite place to travel be if budget were no issue?" Things along those lines are used to spark conversations with your tribe and followers. An important side note—you must engage with the people that are engaging with you.

When someone shares where they would like to travel:
1. Love their comment.

2. Reply back to their comments and ensure that you tag their name in your response. The reason for this is that Facebook gives additional weight currently, at the moment of production of this book, to tags and conversations that happen in an authentic and organic manner.

3. You don't just want to reply thank you. End your response with an open-ended question where you look for information back.

What this also does is create the top of the waterfall that will cascade through the rest of the week. A bit of little known information for you—Facebook engagement is currently the highest on Mondays.

TUESDAY TOO

On Tuesday, we can almost guarantee that any person that commented on our Monday post will also see our first post on Tuesday. That first post on Tuesday should be built around bringing your tribe closer to you. These are typically done in video format, preferably, and should be done using something called spark camera. This app allows for the cut frame type of video that increases watch through time (the key metric for video relatability to your followers in Facebook's eyes).

In order to bring people closer to us, we must share things that bring them inside of our lives. Perhaps it's what our superpower is, or something that we're still working on. Maybe it's a shout out to a close friend, family member, or someone special to us. We're having conversations about our loved ones, or people inside of our business, but you want to ensure that you are ultra-relatable to your ideal client avatar. Also, please keep in mind that as coaches, mentors, and consultants, we often believe that we must have everything figured out. We don't. We are not supposed to. In truth, people most want to buy from people they can relate to. So make sure that your Tuesday posts are very, very relatable. These again should be in video format and should have a small caption that grabs attention.

WEDNESDAY WHAT?

Wednesday's post is about giving away FREE value to the marketplace. The easiest way to establish yourself as an authority figure is by giving away things that most people will charge for. As you do this, this is not something to grab email addresses from. This is a real sharing of things that you know work. It could be something from conversation with a current client. It could be something you have read that you implemented and know works. It could really be anything that adds value to your ideal client avatar's life with nothing expected in return.

This too should be a spark camera video, three minutes or less in length, and should have an attention-grabbing headline and small type above the post. See reference for details.

ACTION THURSDAY

Thursday's posts will be the time in which we now ask for people to take action. We do this on Thursday for a number of reasons. First of all, most people in the world get paid every other Friday, so people are most likely to make a buying decision when they know they are about to get paid. Second, throughout the week, the people that have become most engaged in our content are now the ones that are still seeing what we're sharing. So, the closing percentage for them is going to be much higher. Third, we've established trust, authenticity, and brand awareness prior to putting out something that asks someone to take an action. These posts could consist of inviting people to a private group, inviting people to a low-end offer, inviting people to a mastermind, or inviting people to a case study.

I go very deep into this training inside of The 7 Figure Network Marketer Facebook group. I would love for you to join us (getting tired of me trying to give away value yet? Don't be! I practice what I preach). There is just too much information that is constantly changing about best practices around posting to articulate through a book. It could be a book unto itself (albeit an outdated one before it gets to the printer with the speed of social media these days).

FRIDAY PUMP IT UP

The Friday post ends up being specifically related to what you're looking forward to in the future. Perhaps it's someone you're looking forward to working with, a trip you're taking, a book you're reading, or a course you're creating. This shows an ideal client that we're not just stuck in one position, but that we also care about what's going on moving forward. These too should be videos, three minutes in length or less using spark camera and typed with a small description above the post.

Now for extra credit. To create extra reach I want to share with you a secret I refer to as priming the pump.

When you first wake up every morning, set an alarm clock on your phone, or go to eggtimer.com and set a 15 minute alert. Then, for 15 minutes straight, you're going to hop in your newsfeed and as quickly, but as diligently as you can, you're going to like and comment on posts from your ideal client avatar while tagging the person who posted it on everything you possibly can. Every bit of information, every bit of knowledge, every bit of anything. You want to make sure you can communicate. The exception being sponsored content.

Sponsored content gives no additional weight and it's not worth the time to comment on it. This would also be a great time to start cleaning up your friend feed. I say that because we're going to start treating this profile like a business in itself. In the next chapter, you're going to learn one of the biggest secrets to increasing engagement and increasing reach on Facebook.

IT'S THE WEEKEND!

Saturday and Sunday become free days, days in which you have extra time to post extra content of whatever comes to mind. No matter what, don't forget to prime the pump seven days a week for 15 minutes and like and comment on every post. You can even make a game out of it, and see how many you can get done each day. Over a 30-day period, your reach inside Facebook should more than double instantaneously. If, during the same time, you start eliminating people that will never do business with you and only adding in the ideal clients you want to attract, can you imagine just how quickly your business will grow? I think you're starting to see how we're getting to the $10k a month in recurring revenue.

Action Steps for Content That Matters:

1. Done is better than perfect.

2. Get creative with it.

3. It's NOT about YOU.

4. Be consistent with this.

5. It's going to take 30 days.

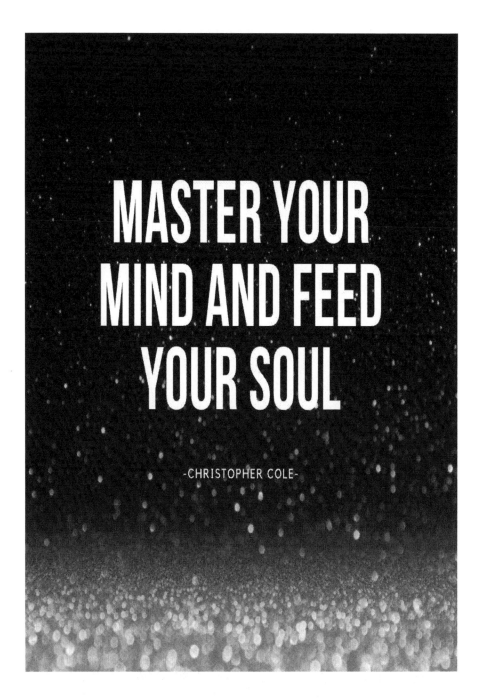

Chapter Seven

Funnel Them In

Group Funnels helps automate the process when collecting information from your groups. It's then integrated into your Google Doc that can then be manually processed or added to a CRM. I told you that you didn't need technology to pull this off, but a CRM will be something to consider investing in for the future. Now, every time someone joins the group, you're able to slowly provide them value through email and build authority, brand, and eventually a brainstorming conversation. You have to connect and follow up with every single person. This is not just about you anymore. It's about them. It's about the impact you can have on the lives of others in the industry, just like the impact I am making on your life. This business is for the service of many. When you have the service of many, it leads to greatness and massive success. You have to be willing to put the success of others first! This will build you, this will attract people to you, and this will change your life forever!

This is a step that can help you build today, tomorrow, and forever. This is a great way to stay engaged with the base that you create. You can find more information on this in my private Facebook Group.
https://www.facebook.com/groups/The7figurenetworkmarketer/

Action Steps for Funnel Them In:

1.) Go to https://www.groupfunnels.com/

2.) Know that you don't need this right away.

3.) It is an investment but worth it.

HOW TO: Collect Data From Your Facebook Group for Future Business. Visit the group funnels website and install the software on your Facebook page. We will have a video on how to do this in the private Facebook group.

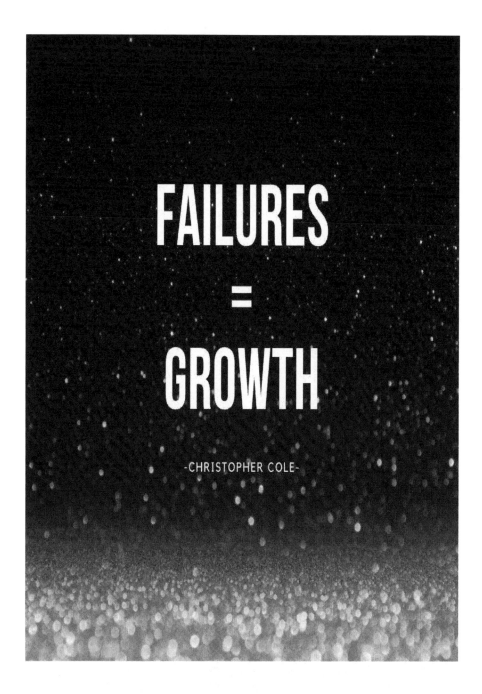

Chapter Eight

It's Going Down In The Dm's

This sequence must be followed exactly. Do not deviate from this under any circumstances or it will not work. This is tried and true and has been proven over and over again. Here's what it looks like. Someone comments, you exchange information, and you end up in their direct message. Now we're going to talk about what we say to them. The flow of this is always consistent. This is a conversation that is for recruiting distributors. You will make slight changes for building your client base.

When you have your ideal client figured out, the conversation will be easier for you. Try to not recruit every single person. If they are interested in your opportunity and do not match up with your ideal client that's okay. Give them the information for an opportunity call but make sure they are willing to become your ideal client by being coachable and doing the work. I wasted a lot of time and effort on those who said they wanted it but they truly didn't. They made excuses or they just wanted to be a spectator.

I go over that in the private Facebook Group.

https://www.facebook.com/groups/The7figurenetworkmarketer/

How To: Best way to have a conversation in the direct message.

"Hey, [person's name]!!!" [Enter]
"I saw your comment on my post." [Enter]
"Thank you so much for the engagement." [Enter]

The reason that we keep sending individual messages is because that's the way that we actually speak. Also, if they're on their phone or on their computer, it will show three separate alerts letting them know there's some urgency here. At that point, we say nothing until they respond. Most people say, "No problem," "Absolutely," or "My pleasure." We want to phrase it in such a way that we put ourselves in the authoritative role. How we do that is with the following.

"Before I share all the details with you…" [Enter]

"Would you mind me asking you a few quick questions so that I can see if you are a good fit for what I have to offer?"" [Enter]

Do not say anything else until they respond. Every person says "Sure," but what you have done is put yourself in the driver's seat with that little line that says, "So I can see if you are a good fit." This also gives you an out at the bottom. Before you present what your offer is, hold back if they do not meet your criteria.

Every person I have ever found says yes. After they say yes, you share.

"Wonderful! Thanks!"

Every time that we ask for feedback from a potential client, we want to praise them. We want to have them feeling like they have done a great thing. We want them mentally feeling like they're seeking our approval. We would start by asking for a success that they have now. If these are already established people, we talk about what that looks like for them.

We'll talk about my industry, coaching. I like to talk about where they want to arrive at first because I want to have them in an elevated emotional state prior to bringing them back down to reality. So I would ask, currently, what is the next rung of the income ladder you're searching to grab on a per month basis? This is a fancy way of saying, "How much money are you trying to make?" People usually answer,

"Well, gosh, I'd really like to get to $10,000 a month." They may have a different dollar amount. That's okay.

My answer is always:

"Beautiful!" or "Excellent!" or "Incredible!"

Then I say,

"I have no doubt you'll get there. The only question is how quickly?"

That's when I instantly jump into the next question.

"Where is your current income sitting?"

They're going to share it. No matter what they share, I say,

"I understand that. That's still really good money though."

Then I put it on them, and I ask,

"So what's the biggest hurdle standing between you and $10,000 per month?" (Or their goal income)

They're going to share whatever they share with you. When they share it, you respond back with:
"I understand."

Most people that I get the opportunity to speak with share something very similar. Respond with:
"I'm very familiar with that."
Then you ask a question.

"Would you like an easy way to get those hurdles out of the way?"

People always say "Yes," right? They've told you their pain point. "I don't know how to generate sales." "I don't know how to generate leads." "I don't know how to close someone." "I don't have enough time."

People always say "yes." The next question we ask is,

"OK, moving those obstacles out of the way. Would you like to wait and do it later or jump on it sooner?"

This is testing someone's wherewithal to jump in to get behind the scenes. Everybody I've ever spoken to says they definitely want to move it out of the way now, and I congratulate them.

"Perfect. I had a feeling you were a quick action taker. That's great! It sounds like you're the perfect fit for my opportunity." [Enter]

You wait for them to get excited, and say "yay" or "good." Then you play takeaway.

"Instead of breaking my thumbs and trying to type in all the details, I've saved the notes of what I have created in a simple overview video." [Enter]

"I hope that's okay." [Enter]

"Are you okay if I send it over to you to look at right now?" [Enter]

Everyone says yes. They've already felt like they've closed a deal. They're almost to the point of being able to get what you have to offer them.

"It's coming right up. But do me a favor. Open it up and read it all the way through." [Enter]

"I'm going to sit here with my chat window open until I hear back or in case you have a question." [Enter]

Then, send them the overview video that your company has created to outline your program. If you'd like more information on how to use this video or create one of your own, join The 7 Figure Network Marketer private group where I break down exactly how to make this happen. This would be an entire book on its own, so instead of trying to cram it into this book, I've created a course for you to be able to digest it in a much easier format. At the end of the overview that you or your company has created, there is always an option to say they're all in to jump into the program. So when someone's watching the overview, all that's left is for them to either ask a question or say I'm in. Let's assume that they say they're all in.

You congratulate them on making a great decision, tell them that's wonderful, and tell them how excited you are.

"Now let's get you quickly enrolled or added to my private Facebook group."

However you get people into your program, maybe you have your own online platform or maybe it's a Facebook group, whatever it is, you want to get them ready. **"By the way, what's the easiest way to pay for whatever the program is? Are you okay if I send you a link right here and wait for you to pay it?"**

People will say "yes," then we must give the link to them at that moment. Then, we sit here and we wait for them to jump in. During this time, I also ask,

"What's your best email address?"

We need their email address now to send them a few consistent documents. Distributor support tools, customer support tools, etc. Whatever your company provides you with.

Every person that decides to work with me also gets an expectation sheet. I tell them that there are thirteen things they can expect from me, and I only expect three in return. That's created to show people that I am bringing more to the table than I require of my clients. Then, depending on the level of service they decide to work with me, they might also get the next year's content calendar. In that, they get invited to the masterminds that we have inside of our private Facebook group. They also get invited to three calls a week that we have to help them progress in their business, and access to other bonuses too.

That's the best way to handle that situation because it shows someone how serious you are about this craft. From there, you can invite them into your group. Hopefully by now, you have a private group specifically for your members inside of Facebook, and you shared a welcome post. You take their picture from their profile, tag them in it, and you share it across the board. You welcome them to the group, get people to comment, and make them feel bonded and like they are a part of the tribe and community. These things create such an impact and they don't require you to pick up the phone.

Action Items for It's Going Down In The DM's:

1.) This takes practice. Take action.

2.) Follow the steps.

3.) You may have to make small changes to fit your opportunity. We can figure it out in the private group.

4.) Don't overwhelm a prospect.

The Six Figure Network Marketer

Chapter Nine

Master Duplicator

If you can't duplicate, then you are alone. I know what you're going through when it comes to duplication. Your team's not growing, I've been there. I've been there quite a few times and have had to rebuild my team. I have had to weed out the people that did not align with my goals. Remember that you're going to go through that process and it's not going to be perfect. It's not going to come together right away. It's going to take time in this business. When your team's not growing, there's no moving up that marketing plan. I am going to help you speed this process up so you don't have to grow your business at a slow pace. When you start getting duplication going, it's going to take off and you can then automate it. You have to create a simple system driven business. Not a people driven business. You can use all the systems I have provided in the chapters before to do that. Teach what I have taught you. That is one simple solution for duplication.

HOW TO: Create a simple system that you and your team can follow and duplicate.

This system may have already been created by your upline or the person that enrolled you.

I am also sure that the company you are a part of has a simple system for you to plug into already. Take the time to find out when weekly calls are going to happen. Every opportunity had an event cycle. Plug yourself and your team into that cycle.

This has been created for a reason. Don't try to reinvent the wheel. Let the leadership help build your team and duplicate them.

Action Items for Master Duplicator:

1.) Fall in love with the process.
2.) Lead from the front.
3.) Follow the system.
4.) If you don't have a system, create one.

Your duplication will depend on your SYSTEM in place. If you have a great system to follow, your team will follow it and the growth will come naturally.

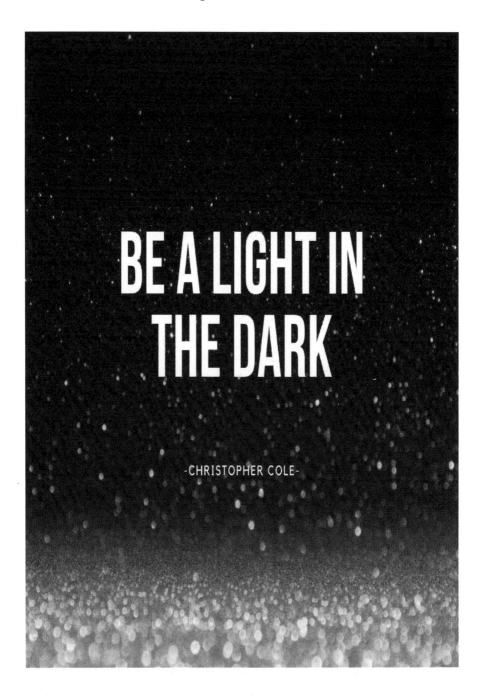

Chapter Ten

BECOME A PRODUCT OF YOUR PRODUCT

Recruit with your product first. You want to make sure that you're not leading with the business. When it comes to duplication, you want to be leading with the product. You want your team to fall in love with the products or service that you are providing. When they do, it will be easier for them to share and duplicate as well. Tell, Show, Teach. You want to be able to teach everything in this book to your team, master it, and keep it simple. Simple systems work best. The simpler you keep it, the better it works. It does not take long to implement these simple secrets into your business.

This is a better way to build your team also because it creates longevity. It makes it more comfortable for your team to share the opportunity with others. It also makes it easier for recruitment to take place on social media because they believe what they can see, not what they hear. It's a big shift from what you may have been taught, but I have seen it grow network marketing businesses faster than leading with the opportunity. I have also seen companies get in trouble because of the fact they lead with the business and are not customer-driven. Imagine having customers that get customers? I am sure after some success, they would rather make the profit than give it to you, which is what you want. And if they want to just be customers, then that's okay also. Let them stay where they feel comfortable.

HOW TO: This is one of the simplest action items you can take when it comes to building your business to $10,000 per month. Become a lover of your product. Truly love your product and always be using it. If you are using the product, you become familiar with it. You know how it works. You know the results you get and you then are able to talk about it more comfortably and confidently. This is something you should not even have to think about when it comes to building your network marketing business and it is most likely the reason you got started in your business in the first place.

I know a lot of people lead with the business opportunity, but if you lead with the products, you can help that new person create a story to sell and they will most likely stay around longer in your business. Some of my best business builders were my personal customers that got a result and then were approached by others about the results they got. They then wanted to make money under me. It works beautifully and it's natural.

This is going to be one of the most important steps that can truly determine the success you are going to have in your network marketing business. If you don't have a product success story then what are you going to share with others? What is going to attract them to you? Also, you are going to feel more confident from getting a result and will most likely be willing to talk about it with others. You will also have people asking you what you have been doing if they have not seen you in a while. This step can determine how serious you are about your network marketing opportunity as well! It will show how committed you are to yourself and your success. So ask yourself... How much do I want this? Am I willing to get uncomfortable so I can obtain the success that I want so badly?

You have to be willing to grow, be coachable, and do what may be different than what you are used to. Maybe you already do it this way and that is great. Now teach your team to do the exact same!

Action Items for Become A Product Of Your Product:

1.) Whatever the product is that you are building with, fall in love with it.

2.) Use the products daily.

3.) Show people you are using the products.

4.) Get a result of some sort from your products.

5.) Document your journey with the products.

6.) Fall in love with that journey.

The Six Figure Network Marketer

Chapter Eleven

AUTOPILOT

Let it rip. Yes, you can get to a place where your business takes off for you. Growing your team and duplicating at a great speed. You have a few options right now. Your first option is you can keep going. You can keep building your network marketing business the way you are. Or, you can make some changes. I know that you can get there if I could get there. I've been where you are. I know what you're going through. I want to help you. I want to change your current situation. Now is the time for you to get to that pivotal six figures in the industry. You have to make a decision to go all in. Make a decision to take massive action. Put your customers first and implement all that I have shared with you.

Like the great Jim Rohn says, "You help enough people get what they want, you will get what you want." I would like to connect with you and help you take it beyond this book. There is so much more to this! I would love to work with you and help you grow your network marketing business. We may not be in the same company or on the same team, but that's what it's all about. It's about helping each other. You can book a free call with me and we can discuss what you're currently going through and what you're dealing with. Then we can brainstorm how to get you past that and grow your team as well.

HOW TO: You are on your way to $10,000 per month. On your way to achieving your goals, you will want to start thinking about how you can put your business on autopilot. I have a solution for that. You are not ready for it just yet, but you will be. It's not hiring an assistant. It's hiring a virtual assistant from another country. You will want to be able to do this when you get to that point. I have an exact way to do that, and you can find it all on my Facebook group page.
https://www.facebook.com/groups/The7figurenetworkmarketer/

Action Steps for Autopilot:

    1.) Join the private Facebook Group for more guidance.

The Six Figure Network Marketer

Chapter Twelve

YOU ARE NOT ALONE ANYMORE

We have arrived at the end of the book. Great job for completing it. You've established the exact framework I have used for myself for getting to six figures in the industry. I have provided you the steps you can take to go from zero to six figures in your network marketing business online. There are so many solutions that can take you to six figures in network marketing. The thing is, you have to be willing to take the steps to make it happen.

The book will continually be updated as technology changes. With the help of The Seven Figure Network Marketer Private Facebook group, you will also be up to speed on the changes and what's coming. We always want to be ready for change and be ahead of the curve. This is an ever changing and evolving industry that is taking off right now! So many people I personally know are doing incredible things inside of the industry. They are paving the way and I want you to become a part of that movement. Stake your claim in the industry.

I truly feel I found the industry because it was meant to be. I have learned so much because of the failures and success that I have had. I have been able to meet some of the best network marketers in the world like Alex

Morton, Ryan Baker, Bill Baker, Nick Sarnicola, Rachael Jackson, Ashley Riggs and the list goes on.

They all have something in common and it's the drive to have an impact on the lives of others. That's what I feel I was truly put here to do and is exactly why I am so excited to share my journey and this book with you. This book brings us all closer.

By now, you should see that this book is a tool that has tremendous value to help you not only get people to join your network marketing opportunity, but also your Facebook group tribe and community. If you have gained value from the book or it has made an impact on your business, message me directly and let me know what you thought about the book. Good or bad. I want to get better and provide as much value as I possibly can to the community. My mission is to help everyone grow and experience success in the network marketing industry.

I heavily encourage you to share it with The 7 Figure Network Marketer Group. Then, we can learn about you and what the book changed for your business. We want to continue to grow and would like to grow with you.

Yes, knowing that you came from the book is extremely important. That way I already know that you have been through the steps of what I have created and we can have a different conversation about furthering your success. That's what this is truly about. Connecting and making sure you have all the success that you have ever wanted.

These steps will work, even if you surpassed $10,000 a month in the network marketing industry. In the group, we will cover more in depth topics on how to continually grow your business and have a greater impact in your community and tribe, all complimentary. We want you to have success. It's what you deserve. I believe we must give more than we receive and always be willing to give to others in order to get what we want out of life. I encourage you to reach out to me so that we can connect. I will make it very easy to do so.

The link to spend more time with me is: https://www.facebook.com/ChristopherCole7figures

I know that one thing is for sure. If you do not make a decision like I did to get a coach, you will be at the same spot you are now. I have learned that you need a coach or mentor of some sort anytime you are trying to level up with anything. They know how to take you to the next level. They challenge you to get uncomfortable. All the success you want is just in your grasp, outside of your comfort zone that you built.

So, I encourage you to take the next step. Be brave. Be confident. Be that leader that you need. Read the book. Do the work. Grind until your dreams come true. Pull others up!

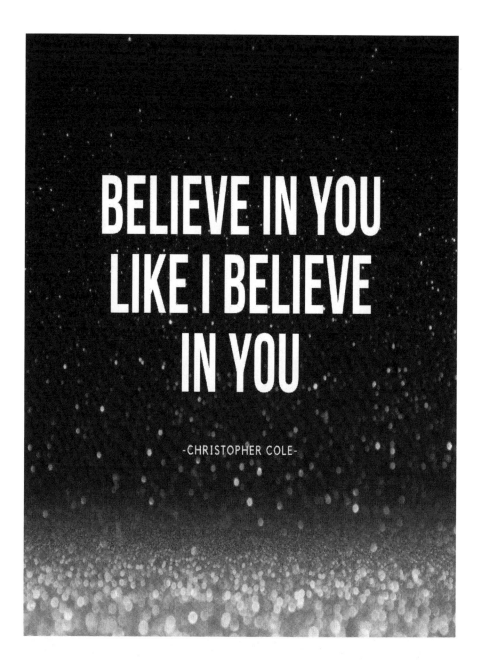

BONUS

YOUR ULTIMATE HACK ACTION ITEMS

It has been a long chapter, but you are here to grow, learn, and make a difference in your network marketing business. Here is a list of your action items from what we have covered so far.

1.) Download <u>friendfilter.io</u> then run it and remove all of your unengaged friends.

2.) Join groups where your ideal clients are located.

3.) Add 20 people from those groups each day.

4.) Make certain to prime the pump every morning before you post.

5.) Have some of the first posts of the day be the most engaging, something like quotes from <u>brainyquotes.com</u>

6.) Make sure that your profile has a:
    Unique profile picture.
    Call-to-action banner and eye-catching description.
    Five great carousel pictures with the first being another call-to-action.

7.) Create a Facebook group that has an easy name to associate with your ideal client.

8.) Make certain the banner on that page covers who should be in that group and the value they're going to receive.

9.) Ensure the group is private.

10.) Ensure the group has three questions in order to join, one of which addresses the client's biggest pain point and one of which is an email capture.

11.) Make certain you have groupfunnels.com running behind the scenes to compile all of that data.

The Six Figure Network Marketer

Your Journey

It's not going to be easy

But it's going to be worth it

You have to decide that you want to be great

You have the unique opportunity and perfect timing to create a business that can create generational wealth that you can leave to your kids. Imagine if your children were able to take over your successful network marketing business and continue to grow it over the world and create a larger impact than you could've ever imagined. With the changes that are taking place, skill is becoming more important than a college degree. You could set your children up for massive success. They could develop into some of the best leaders in and out of the industry. I say this because the skills we have to learn as we grow in this industry are some of the most character-building skills of any industry. You are your own boss so you have to develop leadership, self-leadership, focus, drive, passion, and so much more to set yourself apart and do well. The skills I have learned over the years because of the industry have forever changed my life and the way I live my life! We are taught how profits are better than wages. How you can create the life you have always wanted. How you can be happy working a business you love! How life doesn't have to be tied to a desk. That life can be built to your standards and can be lived the way you choose to live it. A life by design if you will.

I still get so fired up about the fact that in this industry, we can travel and work whenever we choose to. With hard work and dedication, you can make all your dreams come true. You can create the life you have always dreamed of. Doing the normal thing is not required anymore. It's time to set yourself FREE of mediocrity. It's TIME to become who you were truly meant to be!

The only catch is YOU! You have to want to do that. You have to want to put in the work. You have to want to show up when times are tough and you feel like giving up. YOU HAVE TO REMEMBER WHY YOU STARTED!

You have to have that burning desire inside to control the direction of your life. You deserve it!

I can help guide you, but I can't find you. You have to find me and connect!

With that being said, I leave you with this.

One of the biggest waves ever is happening right now in network marketing. Something I have never seen before and we don't know if we will see it ever again in our lifetime. Don't make the decision to sit on the fence and not put what I shared with you in the book to action.

You have an amazing opportunity in front of you. Don't look back and regret the lack of decision that can haunt you forever.

"We must all suffer from one of two pains: the pain of discipline or the pain of regret. The difference is discipline weighs ounces while regret weighs tons." -Jim Rohn

Take Action Today

"Do Not Give Your Past The Power To Define Who You Are." -Dhiren Prajapati

We have a lot more in common than you may even realize. I share a little bit of my story in the beginning of the book but I wanted to really take the time to connect with you in this last section. I wanted to share with you that I struggle with depression and I often self-sabotage, but writing this book has been one of the most freeing and inspiring things I have done so far in my life. I never thought I would be able to accomplish this, but I did, thanks to a great team and group of friends that believed in me.

I deal with an inner voice, perhaps just like you, that says you are not good enough for success. But I want to tell you that you can change that voice, just like I did. With consistent work on your inner self, you can make a change and have everything you want and deserve. You are worthy of being at the top of your company. You are worthy of becoming a network marketing great. You are worthy of love, success, time and so much more!

Own it! Believe it! See it everyday for yourself and your

team!!

Don't let all the decisions you made in the past define who you are in this industry. It's a fresh start and you can start today! You can be the change you so badly need in your life. You are the author of your LIFE. We owe it to ourselves to write how our lives are lived and you can live the life of your DREAMS!

I went from nothing to the amazing human I always knew and wanted to be. I overcame so many obstacles and you may have more obstacles than I have had but just know that people before you did it, so WHY NOT YOU?

FOR THOSE WHO JUST FLIPPED TO THE BACK OF THE BOOK THIS MESSAGE IS FOR YOU!

Don't be lazy and go to the end right away. Make your dreams come true in the network marketing industry just like so many before you. Do the work! Take the inner journey to grow yourself and become the leader that you know you have wanted to be all of your life. Be the type of person you want on your team. Be the top 1% person in your company that you know that it needs! Don't take shortcuts and skip all the fun parts that develop you into the amazing human that you are becoming! KEEP PUSHING! Now go read the whole book because I want to hear your success story one day. MAKE IT HAPPEN! Speak with you soon my friend.

Network marketing saved my life. It has the ability to take you from nothing to something. Don't take it lightly.

Making the decision to get serious in the industry changed my life. I went from partying every weekend to sharing my story on stage in front of over 30,000 people. I believe in YOU! Let's GO!

Made in the USA
Middletown, DE
28 August 2020